THOUGHT
SYSTEMS

How Progressive Professionals
Nurture Their Wisdom

TRACY MCNEIL

TracyMac Publishing
A Division of Peace Place LLC
P.O. Box 767
Knightdale, North Carolina 27545

The author of this book does not offer medical advice or prescribe the use of any technique as a form of treatment for physical or mental challenges without the advice of a physician, either directly or indirectly. The information in the book reflects a portion of the author's spiritual, professional life and personal life experiences and is not intended to replace professional medical or psychological advice. The intent of the author is to assist professionals with interpersonal relationship effectiveness and relationship management. In the event you use any of this information for yourself, the author and publisher assume no responsibility for you actions.

References:
Page 73 and 164, The Message is quoted: "Psalms 23" and Proverbs 3: 13-18 is taken from The Message. Copyright © 1993, 1994, 1995, 1996, 2000, 2001, 2002. Used by permission of NavPress Publishing Group.

United: Thoughts on Finding the Common Ground and Advancing the Common Good by Cory Booker, Copyright 2016, Publisher: Random House Books, New York, Ballentine Books

Interior Design: TWA Solutions (www.twasolutions.com)
Cover Design: Owen McNeil – Another McNeil Creation
Photography: Kisha Lee – Purpose Productions and Photography

ISBN-10: 0-9891013-5-5
ISBN-13: 978-0-9891013-5-6
Library of Congress Control Number: 2016901484

McNeil, Tracy A.
Thought Systems: How Progressive Professionals Nurture Their Wisdom/Tracy A. McNeil and Jayda S. McNeil

First Edition

Printed in the United States of America

Distributed by Ingram Book Group

Dear Wisdom,
I thank you.

ACKNOWLEDGEMENT

I want to thank God for any portion of wisdom I have. I thank my husband of twenty-two years, Owen, and our daughter, Jayda. Their support goes beyond the norm and I receive it as a gift to treasure. I love you forever and like you for always. I thank my parents, Thomasine Rawls Jones and Walter E. Jones Sr., for their supportive prayers and for appreciating my oddities. I love you two, together or apart. I'm grateful for my friends—old, new, past, and present—and my most intimate relationships that have remained consistent, outliving my focus during all the times I chose work over friendship. I'm thankful for my extended family who may not give a damn about what I do professionally, but they gift me with the art of balance, to give and receive love that isn't always spoken, and laughter that should be illegal!

I want to thank the coaching profession for giving me a title in 2004 that would allow me to combine all of my talents, skills, gifts, experiences, and abilities to serve well, get certified, and get paid to do what I love! I'm grateful for every client I've ever had and will have. Thank you for investing in yourself and investing in me. Continue to be great and do great things! I appreciate all my affiliations and networking groups, particularly, my Strategic Alliance Coaching Firm, Coaches Training Alliance (CTA), Eckerd College & Mediation Training Institute International (MTI), professional Black Life Coaches Network, Women On The Move and my local chambers of commerce. I thank Andrea Harris, senior fellow at NCIMED, for being a fascinating leader for women and minorities, who uses her wisdom, hard work, and tenacity have helped change government policy, which positively affects us all.

I also want to thank anyone who underestimated me, including myself. Thank you. It was a gift.

May we all continue to live on purpose, through mission, and with passion! Always remember to be kind, be authentic, be excellent, be generous, and while you're at it, go ahead and be extraordinary!

TABLE OF CONTENTS

FOREWORD

Andrea Harris
Co-Founder & Senior Fellow, The Policy Center

In his *Discourse on the Method*, René Descartes offered the philosophical proposition that "I think, therefore I am." Quite simplistically, he inferred that if you existed there had to be thought, and that to doubt your own existence was not possible as the thought in and of itself meant that you existed. According to *Merriam-Webster*, the word "progressive" means *of, or related to, or showing advancement or taking gradually or step by step*. So, what is all of this about *Thought Systems and Progressive Professional Wisdom*?

In this book, Tracy McNeil offers almost daily statements for reflection and introspection borne out of her own experiences or those of others whom she has coached. Tracy's coaching is a coaching for personal growth and professional development. We all need this type of reflection whether in the professional work place, with family, or just for our own better understanding of ourselves. Moreover, introspection and reflection offer a clear step-by-step intuitive pathway to greater peace of mind.

9

Some may well think of progressive thought in today's political environment. Conceptually, this is not where Tracy wants us to go. She wants us to step away from the politics and correctness of today, and step away from the twists of how we make every concept fit into the box we desire for our own selfish gains. This book offers questions, statements by others, religious verses, and simply thoughts that cause us to talk to ourselves and listen to ourselves. Listening to ourselves, as well as others, is how we grow. But, it is also how we get to better know our own values, build our own character, learn from our own experiences, and nurture and share our wisdom.

My hat is off to Tracy McNeil, the professional life coach, in encouraging and valuing thought and the need to take time to think. Of equal importance is the recognition that the thought process can be progressive. The knowledge from that process, that experience, provides a tool for the discernment of what is right, and just, and good. We should run to embrace any pathway that leads us there. Keep Coaching TRACYMAC!

About Andrea Harris

As Co-Founder & Senior Fellow, Andrea is responsible for the creation of a Policy Center within the Institute with a primary focus on business development and higher education. The Policy Center (TPC) will also function with the guidance, advice, and assistance of a Board of Economic Policy

Advisors. Stepping down after providing 30 years of leadership as the Institute's President, she now devotes her time and energy on issues impacting the minority business community, workforce development and Historically Black colleges and Universities (HBCUs) to name a few. Her strong commitment and work towards building the asset base within low-wealth sectors of the population of our state, has generated numerous awards and recognition for her efforts. She continues to give of her time and talent by sitting on numerous boards and commissions. Andrea is a graduate of Bennett College.

PREFACE

The first time I recall hearing about wisdom was when I was a little girl. I was sitting in church, looking up at Mom. She was always dressed with such sophistication, from head to toe, in what looked to be worthy of 1977 Ebony Fashion Fair. She was always pretty, and dressed nice, but on Sunday, she looked like a beauty queen. She was a fashionista before her time, yet modest. I would look at her and feel rather cute myself. My freshly straightened hair, after the Saturday night brawl we had between my thick afro, a smoking hot straightening comb, and a jar of Blue Magic hair grease, was so straight it looked wet. One wouldn't know that I cried half the day it took her to shampoo, plait, allow drying time, and straighten my hair. One wouldn't have had a clue how tired I got from holding my head down and wincing at the sizzling sound of the hot comb and grease combined with hair that wasn't quite dry. She straightened hair around my temples and hair on the back of my neck I didn't know I had, that no one could see but her. You would have had no idea that I slept in paper bag rollers, helped pick out my matching barrettes and bows as we ran late for church on some Sunday mornings. It was as if all that painstaking preparation was forgotten because we worked together to get right for Sunday's service.

I smoothed out my yellow, polyester dress across my lap to make sure I was straight, too, while looking down at my white, laced, ankle socks and shiny, black, patent leather shoes, watching my well-oiled, puny, chocolate legs swing from the pew. Mom was pretty and after our wrestling match with my hair the night before, I was cute!

You couldn't tell me anything! Not so much about how I looked, but I had a purse! All I could think about was the peppermint candy and the quarter Mom had given me to put in my little, black, patent leather purse. With a frayed strap, I could never seem to keep the snap closed, but that didn't matter. I had a purse! It held my miniature New Testament Gideon Bible, a short, knife-sharpened No. 2 pencil, a few crayons, an old, folded church program, and some old candy wrappers, which were about all I could stuff inside it. I would watch the choir march in. I could sing harmony and I liked to switch up signing the harmonic parts with the choir. Singing alto was my favorite. Though, on occasion, I was still a little scared when folks "caught the Holy Ghost," especially Mom. I was thinking, *Oooh, you're going to mess up your hair and your makeup*. As a child, I enjoyed watching people shout, from a distance, and do what we called the holy dance. However, I knew as soon as all of that took place, I could put my shiny quarter in the offering plate as it passed, or Mom may even let me walk her offering up to the front to put it in one of the baskets. After that, I could have my peppermint! I thought it was a treat, but I think Mom used it to keep me from asking so many questions.

I was a very quiet child, but whenever I had a question, I'd ask! Asking a question during the sermon didn't go over well though, you *had* to be quiet or Mom would say, "Shh! Keep still, Tracy!" I learned quickly to keep my questions *and* keep still. If you didn't, you would get a pinch, and you'd better not cry. Man! The seventies were rough! I didn't like pinches and for damn sure didn't like when she or any other trusted church member would pinch and turn. I was a fast learner, so I didn't have to hear "Keep still, Tracy!" but a few times. I kept still and kept quiet. I would get so bored listening to the sermons. It seemed to take so long, as if hands on the big clock at the back of the church were turning backward. Once that peppermint dissolved, my stomach would start asking, *When are we going to go home and eat?* I wanted to ask out loud, but I had to weigh my options and thought about a possible pinch, and thankfully, the preacher would finally get to the good part. I would always think (and still do) why doesn't he or she just start at the good part? The good part is when the organist or pianist begins to chime in, with gospel chords, an inviting rhythm, and exciting modulations to encourage hype into the message. It would also let the congregants know it was time to close and have altar call. People would stand, leap, and a good preacher could sing his sermon, and if really good, he or she could move the crowd just by saying and singing, "Say yes!" I would wonder, *What are we saying yes to? Do we ever say no?* (The mind of a child.) Until that part, enduring a sermon had hardships— keeping quiet and physically. Those pews were hard.

I remember a time when the church introduced "children's church." It was much like Sunday school, except someone, most times a woman, would gather all the children and take us to the back of the church, the foyer, or outside during the sermon. The church we went to at the time was a small church, with no classrooms, no basement, and no multipurpose room. The teacher would have us sit on the back pew or on the front steps of the church and tell us Bible stories. I liked that. That meant I didn't have to worry about getting pinched or a pinch and turn. I could ask a question! I liked hearing stories about Noah and the ark, Daniel and the lion's den, and Joseph and his coat of many colors. One of the first stories I recall hearing about was of King Solomon. It was the most influential Bible story to me then, and it still is. With my yellow dress, that little black, patent leather purse, matching shoes, and white, laced socks, I was glad to walk Mom's offering up to the front because I was so excited about children's church, I bypassed her pew and went straight to the back. I was ready!

When the teacher told us about the story of King Solomon, found in 1 Kings 3, he was said to have been the wisest. At that age, I used to open my Bible and hunt for all the words I could read: *the, thee, and*—you get the picture. I remember pulling out my little, red, Gideon Bible, trying to find the story, not knowing all I had was the New Testament, and his accounts were in the Old Testament. As I listened intently, finding *my* words didn't matter. This story amazed me! As the story goes, in summary, King Solomon had to decide between two women and one baby. Both women claimed to be the mother of the child. Of course, only one could be real the mother and the other was a liar. With both women seeming to be believable, he suggested to cut the baby in half. My youthful questions pinged like a pinball machine. Why would a mommy lie? Why would the king want to kill a baby? Why didn't he ask the women who was lying? Why didn't he make them share? Why didn't he give the baby to an orphanage? How did he know what to do? With patience to listen, the children's church teacher said, "King Solomon was the wisest man. He had wisdom." I asked, "What's wisdom?" I can't remember her full answer, but I remember it had to do with him being more than just smart. I know her answer had to be good because my next question was, "How do you get it? May I have some, too? She said, "All you have to do is ask God for it." I did. I asked!

It was much later, when I was a teenager, that I remember reading the New Testament writings of James who wrote, "If any man lacks wisdom, let him ask." Something about wisdom made me feel I didn't have to ask God for anything else, but if I had wisdom, there wouldn't be anything else I'd need to ask for because I'd know how to have whatever I needed or desired. Wisdom became intriguing and important to me. I began to understand that wisdom was more than things or being smart or intelligent. It is in innate and applied brilliance. After all, Solomon was able to take that dilemma; he didn't have access to DNA testing, never accused either woman of lying, and didn't need a focus group, a jury, survey, or a team. He didn't test the market, know the valuation, have to integrate platforms, embarrass either woman, or have to destroy the life of a child. He simply said, "Bring me a sword…" and the truth came out quick! The passage further states that all feared him because of his wisdom. Feared? I didn't want anyone to fear me, and I didn't want to fear anybody.

My childhood memory of wisdom—presented with situations that required me to use wisdom, and being aware of the absence of it—is why I decided to write this book. Professionals need wisdom. Leaders need wisdom. We need wisdom in our personal lives, our relationships, our careers, our health, and in our social, financial, political, and religious experiences. Now more than ever, we all need wisdom! We tend to see the world how we see ourselves. When we assess the state of the world, there are a lot of problems. Problems require solutions. Solutions require design, practical strategies, methodical genius, creativity and innovation, all held together by wisdom. Some of the issues like racism, sexism, family and workplace dysfunction, political mayhem, abuse, oppression, unfair economic conditions, hunger, and ongoing wars will not be solved using a textbook, a pie chart, algorithms, reports, marketing, a social media ad, or even a religious tradition.

You would think common sense would handle it, but common sense isn't so common. What makes sense to some may seem stupid as hell to another. Wisdom facilitates agreement. In some cases, a miracle is the only solvent, but in every situation, wisdom must be present. What's worse than not solving the problem, solving wrong problem or causing the problem, is being too out of touch to realize there is one. We are a quirky lot, yet we are incredible, and have access to every resource necessary to discover solutions to every problem we face. But, the solutions hinge on wisdom. Though I will never claim to understand the brain or the mind, or profess to be the wisest, by far, I do understand the power of the mind and I do have wisdom. I asked and I received. You have it, too. We have to commit to nurture it.

I understand that your mind is the power source of your life. I understand there are systems that can determine how our thoughts function. I understand that you are not your thoughts, but you are the one who sees them. So don't be threatened by your thoughts or anyone else's. Don't be afraid to make your thoughts powerful and positive. On the other hand, don't be intimidated by what you think people think of you, especially when all they are doing is thinking. Now let's be clear. I'm writing to you about thoughts. Just because you think about something doesn't mean you believe it, or believe in it. Thoughts are the foundations and the bridge to beliefs. Beliefs are opinions and convictions in the truth, or the existence of something not immediately susceptible to rigorous proof.

Most things we believe are not because they have been proven true, but because they are simply the first things we were taught, the first things we thought. Evidence that a thought becomes a belief is when the cognitive content is held as true, and is usually supported by action and when the mental act, condition, or habit of placing trust or confidence in another. So until we believe it, it is simply thought.

Take for instance, I can think about people who worship Krispy Kreme Doughnuts and I may even like Krispy Kreme Doughnuts, and I do, but it does not mean I believe in worshipping Krispy Kreme Doughnuts. I can think about a Krispy Kreme Doughnut and it doesn't mean I believe in them or that I am one. My dad, Bishop Water E. Jones, used to say from the pulpit: *"You can't stop a bird from flying over your head (thought), but you can certainly keep it from building a nest in your hair (belief)."*

Thoughts come and go (flight), but when you decide to allow them to take root (nest architecture) they can become beliefs. Your thoughts are where it begins, but believing is when you support them enough to allow them to take root and affect your behavior. As a progressive professional and a leader, your thought life is where it all begins. Whether leaders are born or made, progressive leaders think successfully. They also think positively and, though you're the only one who sees your thoughts, what your thoughts produce can become evidence, tangible or intangible, and potentially experienced by everyone you connect with, personally and professionally.

As a progressive professional, it's not that anyone can give you wisdom, yet, questions, thoughts, principles, and questions can spark, increase, train, and cause wisdom to blossom and increase. In order to be successful and fulfilled, wisdom is required. Wisdom promotes and optimizes your thought processes. Why would one need to nurture their wisdom? Why is wisdom so important? Wisdom separates the experts from the average, excellent from good, denies ignorance, and guides best practices and implements ideal choices. Wisdom is the ability or result of an ability to think and act, utilizing a combination of intuition, accumulated knowledge, experience, understanding, common sense, and insight to enlighten.

To support individual and team self-discovery, professional development and organizational effectiveness, I work with executive staff, business owners, thought leaders, higher education professionals, and social and spiritual change influences, and what I know for sure, as a professional, education and experience are preferred, implemented knowledge is power, but wisdom is required! Considering diversities, gender, race, most businesses consist of Baby Boomers, Generation

X, Generation Y (Millenniums) in the same workspace, and Generation Z (Boomlets) will soon become a part our workforce, all of which have their own thoughts, different belief systems, and personal core values. Wisdom is required to create, accept and drive necessary change and promote functionality and effectiveness.

What can professionals use to nurture their wisdom and embolden the intuition that it takes to design and manage those relationships successfully? Everything is about design and management. What challenges their thought systems to embrace diversity and inclusion and normalize change to keep them from stifling advancement, choking out innovation, and hindering pragmatic solutions?

Successful professionals who lead fulfilled lives:

- Nurture their wisdom and intuition, which fosters encouragement

- Confront and shift stagnant mind-sets

- Challenge archaic beliefs to welcome ingenuity

- Support action on how to drive change that modifies corresponding behaviors.

You may or may not realize when wisdom is present with your thoughts, but you know, without a doubt, when wisdom is absent. You know when friends and family situations are void of wisdom and thought systems are broken and dysfunctional. Yet, some of us carry on accepting it as the norm, which is unnecessary. We have the ability to use wisdom to repair, upgrade, and change, and even destroy negative thought systems that affect our quality of life. Do you know that friend or relative? They say if you don't know who they are, it could be you, and that's for you to determine.

As a professional, have you ever worked for or with someone and you know they are educated, they have been in the profession for quite some time, but you know they lack the ability to put it altogether? They don't have people skills or intuition, they are ineffective, poor decision makers and have no cohesive flow of thought and sometimes their smart seems dumb, or they think you are. Their lack of wisdom can negatively influence a work environment, and depending on how influential they are, they can destroy progress of an entire workforce.

I worked for an agency once, and it was the worst experience I'd ever had in my life. For nearly thirty years, I have worked with all men, all women, and alongside military personnel. I worked in Japan with Japanese Local Nationals, been employed by federal, state and local governments, non-profits, corporate, a day care and have I have volunteered for veterans and with church folks. Working for this one particular agency was like working in a lukewarm hell. It was horrible and sickening. Poor management, underappreciated, overworked, underpaid employees, unfair treatment, no opportunity for training or advancement, biased work conditions, and the absence of wisdom caused by erratic thought systems. The absence of wisdom and broken thought systems is why people quit. I was so grateful to resign! I loved my coworkers, but I had to leave that warped, management groupthink and system of thought. There we so many instances where they tried to suppress thinking, or should I say pretend as if they didn't know you could think. I have so many stories about that place, but I'll use wisdom and "Shh! Keep still, Tracy."

INTRODUCTION

When we talk about systems, most professionals understand business systems. Most understand them to be processes, a procedure, or event using several steps or activities, with the purpose of reaching a goal. The results of a business system are referred to as functionality. Business systems include: customer service, purchasing, sales conversion, hiring, inventory, website, training, operations, shipping, accounting, information systems, payroll, safety, etc. You get the picture. Within the systems are standard operating procedures.

Do you see the gears on this book cover? Have you ever felt that is what the inside of your mind looks like? All of these little systems—like gears—uploading and downloading information, processing and are constantly being expected to work in sync. Some days you're like a well-oiled machine, firing on all cylinders—all systems go! Some days, one gear is moving a little faster, maybe because another gear is tired, no longer working properly or just quit. Other days they're all moving in slow motion. There may even be times you'd like all of them to pause for just a moment. If only you could put the world on pause...

We have so many voices shouting at us and vying for our time, attention, and money it's a wonder we can think. Or, are we thinking? Are we in touch with our thoughts, or are we simply behaving robotically according to external demands and cues? After all, there's everything from the news, reality TV, social media, the fashion world, sports, the entertainment industry, the world of health and fitness, and let's not forget about our money, professions, friends and families, hopefully, not necessarily in that order. How often do we consistently get in touch with our thoughts, put the world on pause to think? When we do think, what are our thoughts? What influences them? Your thoughts are the governing body for the ecosystem of your entire life! Progressive professionals are keen and understand the necessity of wisdom and the power in nurturing it. A progressive professional is one who shows great skill in a given activity or livelihood in a career, who is moving forward or onward, toward development, improvement, and advancement by continuing and steadily in increments. Is that you? If so, keep reading. This is for you. If not, keep reading, you'll learn something, anyway!

Now, let's look at what a thought and a system are, simplistically. Thought is the act or process of thinking, deliberation, or reflection of a concept, opinion, or idea. A system is a group or combination of interrelated, interdependent, or interacting elements forming a collective entity, a methodical or coordinated assemblage of parts, facts, and concepts. So, let's put it all together: *Thought Systems* are the interrelated, interdependent, or interacting elements that we use in the process of thinking, deliberation, or reflection of a concept, opinion, or idea. Simple! What are these interacting elements? What do we think about them? How do we use them? It would be a disservice to your brilliant mind for me to describe or expound upon what *your* thought systems mean

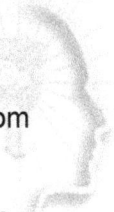

to you, or how you think. I have no idea what you think. So, for the sake of continuity, I will share, what I believe, are some of our *Thought Systems*.

Your wisdom is nurtured by how well you connect and intertwine these systems and how you determine a most accurate course of action, based upon those calculated results. I'd simply like to challenge you to be aware of what they are, how you feel about them, how they affect your wisdom and every relationship you will ever have with a noun. One way to challenge without being offensive or bias is to ask thought provoking questions. Questions allow you to answer intimately, but know that your answers will reveal your thoughts and ultimately influence your behavior. Systems of thought can include:

- Family & Upbringing
- Race & Culture
- Sexuality & Sensuality
- Religious Expression & Sacred Interpretations
- Money & Finances
- Social & Friendships
- Academic
- Professional
- Entertainment & Fashion
- Technology & Social Media

Of course, this is not an exhaustive list, yet it does cover the bases. Depending on their niche and level of expertise, the questions within each system are the kinds of questions you may experience in a professional coaching session. Life coaching niches include: personal life, relationships, business and branding, career, sales, executive and leadership and health and wellness. Though authentic coaching may feel therapeutic, any reputable and professional coach understands they are *not* a therapist or a licensed counselor, and does not use the session to treat a crisis, deal with mental illness, or heightened levels of dysfunction, nor attempt to engage in any medical diagnosis whatsoever. They understand therapy and counseling is more like archeology, where the patient digs, and coaching is architecture, where the client builds. Through "building questions," coaching may require turning some soil to determine the quality of the foundation that has been laid for the structure being built. Ideal clients desire personal discovery or professional development to be more successful, effective, satisfied and fulfilled, and construct their own answers. They want to create, excel, discover, and achieve big and bigger goals and they choose not to go it alone.

During a session, a coach does not showcase their wisdom because that may only last as long as the session. But, an effective coach uses their wisdom to intentionally create a judgment free zone, pose stimulating questions that will support and challenge you discover your own wisdom, that way you have it for life. As you engage, by answering the following questions, it would be beneficial to you to record your answers. Doing so will allow you to slow down for a moment, put the world on pause, to see what you're thinking…really thinking. It can serve as a way to expose your pattern of thought, reveal areas you haven't given much thought to, showcase your genius, and privately admit ignorance. You can further use them delve into the layers of your "how's" and "whys."

Because your wisdom is the culmination of your excellent systems of thought, it is imperative that you answer these questions to nurture it further. See these *Thought Systems* as the gears and each question is like the teeth and grooves that fit together and turn, productively. Operating properly, it produces and enhances wisdom. Think of it as if wisdom is the oil that optimizes cohesion, synchronicity, and synergy. Be patient with yourself as you answer, as this may be the first time you've thought about some of these questions or taken time to answer.

System 1 - Family & Upbringing

1. How do you define family? Marriage? Children? Think about divorce? The unmarried?
2. What are your definitions based upon?
3. How were you raised?
4. What role did women play in how you were raised?
5. What role did men play in how you were raised?
6. What did you enjoy most about your childhood?
7. What did you enjoy the least about your childhood?
8. How important is family to you?
9. What role do you play in your definition of family?
10. How well do you play it?

System 2 - Race & Gender

1. How do you feel about racism?
2. What do you think about your own race?
3. What do you think about other races?
4. How well do you embrace racial and cultural differences?

5. What affect do you think racism or sexism has had in our life?
6. What are your thoughts about your own gender?
7. What are your thoughts about the opposite sex?
8. How do you feel about gender role assignment?
9. How have you been affected by the opposite sex?
10. How have you affected the opposite sex?

System – 3 Sexuality & Sensuality
1. What do you think about sex?
2. Who taught you about sex?
3. What are you basing your sexual opinions and beliefs on?
4. What makes them right?
5. How do your morals and values affect your sexuality?
6. What are your thoughts about heterosexuality?
7. What are your thoughts about homosexuality?
8. How comfortable are you with your sensuality?
9. How much influence does the media have on your sensual appetite?
10. How can you improve your sexual health?

System 4 - Religious Expression & Sacred Interpretations
1. Who is God to you?
2. Who first taught you about religion? What was that like?
3. What are your current religious beliefs?
4. How do you feel about religion as a whole?
5. How much credence do you give clergy?
6. How have your thoughts toward religion evolved or changed?

7. How do you handle personal or professional relationships that have different beliefs?
8. How literal do you embrace text you deem sacred?
9. What is the ideal role of religion?
10. How much of what you think about religion is solely based on tradition?

System 5 – Money & Finances

1. What do you think about money?
2. How well do you handle money?
3. How do you think money works?
4. How healthy are your finances?
5. What was your best financial experience?
6. How do you feel about giving and helping others?
7. How often do you talk about money?
8. What can you do to improve your finances?
9. What does financial planning mean to you?
10. How much does money factor into your overall happiness?

System 6 – Social & Friendships

1. How do you make friends (personal and professional)?
2. How does quantity or quality affect your friendships?
3. What kinds of social groups are you in (formal and informal)?
4. How well do you interact and connect with other people?
5. How diverse are your social groups (race, age, gender, religious, economic)?

6. Why are you a part of your particular social groups? Network groups?
7. How affected are you by groupthink?
8. What do you bring to your social groups?
9. What do you receive from your social groups?
10. How do social groups support you?

System 7 – Academic

1. What has been your experience with academia?
2. How important is education?
3. What forms of education are most important to you?
4. How has education helped or hindered you?
5. How has your education influenced your life?
6. What subject matter feels most natural?
7. What subjects have proven to be most challenging?
8. How do you learn best?
9. How important are institutions of higher learning?
10. How do your support continuing your academic growth?

System 8 – Professional

1. Why did you choose your current profession?
2. How satisfied are you with your job?
3. What are your professional achievements?
4. Where do see yourself with in the next three years?
5. What are your short-term professional goals?
6. What support do you need to achieve them?
7. How do feel about your employer or employees?
8. How relevant is your profession?
9. What other professions do you find attractive?
10. How can you optimize and be more innovative?

System 9 – Entertainment & Fashion

1. How much does the entertainment world influence your realty?
2. How involved are you in sports entertainment?
3. How much time do you invest in entertainment?
4. How much emphasis do you place on fashion?
5. What is your preferred form of entertainment?
6. How has entertainment been harmful?
7. How has entertainment been helpful?
8. How can you use entertainment to your advantage?
9. What do you contribute to the entertainment industry, or to the fashion world?
10. How does the importance of entertainment and fashion in your relationships affect you?

System 10 – Technology & Social Media

1. How does technology affect your personal life?
2. How does technology affect your professional life?
3. How does technology support convenience?
4. What is your social media life like?
5. How influenced are you by social media?
6. How has technology and social media affected your closest relationships?
7. How much time do you spend on social media?
8. What is technology best used for?
9. How has technology been a hindrance, personally or professionally?
10. How do you influence technology and social media?

Are there more systems of thought? Of course! I just believe these ten along with the one hundred questions are a great place to spark thought toward nurturing your wisdom. A simple way to get those gears turning and keep them well oiled! I also want to support nurturing your wisdom. Nurture simply means to promote development, to feed support, train, or education and to inspire with confidence and give hope and courage. That's where the wisdom principles come in. The principles I share with you are designed to inspire confidence and give hope and courage. They can encourage the initiation of internal and external communication, cultivate relationships, increase confidence, creativity and balance commitment.

Your thoughts affect your quality of life, and progressive professionals must use their minds for more than just static echo chambers. Systems of thought, as a progressive and leader, require education, knowledge, experience, and wisdom, and it not only affects you, but the lives of those you lead.

WISDOM
PRINCIPLES

WISDOM PRINCIPLES

A s you delve into the principles, consider your thought systems. Sometimes the one(s) that screams the loudest is the bully and needs the least consideration. Society really doesn't want you to think, they want to think for you, think ahead of you, tell you what to think and you behave accordingly, effortlessly. There's something about wisdom or philosophy that can make even the most intelligent mind feel as though they need a decoder. You'll find these principles are pragmatic.

My prayer for you:

Think your thoughts as loud as you like, you're the only one who hears them.

Make them as colorful as you choose, you're the only one who paints them.

Allow them to be as pleasurable as you desire, you're the first one who feels them.

Create them to be as incredible as you dare because others will see you be them.

Design your thoughts a positive as you can so that wisdom will help you nurture them.

HOW TO GET THE MOST
OUT OF THE WISDOM PRINCIPLES

✓ Read aloud.

✓ Be aware of your thought systems as you read and manage your mind-set.

✓ Make a deliberate choice to confront your thoughts, not like a bully but as an ally.

✓ Have journal handy.

✓ It may be helpful to read a quote or two and close the book.

✓ Write down principles that you embrace wholeheartedly and place them in places that nurture your wisdom and spark encouragement (mirrors, screen savers, etc.)

✓ Have an open mind and be open to change

✓ Don't be afraid to embrace a new thought or discard one that no longer serves you well.

✓ Suppress your social media habits, don't simply scroll.

✓ Think of a real-world experience that either confirms, challenges or refutes each quote, and behave accordingly. When applicable, enjoy implementing a principle that may invite and support solutions.

✓ Engage in conversations about a principle that resonates with you and feel free to share your reading experience with your family, friends, colleagues, workgroups or employees.

It's not the size of the goal, it's how big you do it!

⚮

Trusting the whispers of your "first mind" eliminates
the argumentative mistakes of second guessing.
Trust you!

⚮

It's not so much that a good man or good woman is
hard to find, they are too often overlooked.

⚮

What are you enough for?

39

Self-discovery is the beginning of internal alignment. Self-discovery isn't a time when you begin to think so much of yourself that it invites selfishness or arrogance. It is an intentional process of realizing who you are so that you and everyone you are connected to knows who they are getting. Who are they getting?

"The best teachers are those that show you where to look, but don't tell you what to see."
—Alexandra K. Trenfor

❧

Sexism grooms cowards. Racism is applauded by ignorance. Greed produces lunatics. You don't have to guess. You already know how and who. You are also intelligent enough to do something great about changing it. Now!

❧

Play hard. Dance to your own beat. Sing without music. Smile freely. Laugh loud. Repeat often!

Purpose doesn't give you things, you give things purpose.

How long will you continue to live up to their expectations and fail at yours? God gave YOU these pages of life to write, who has your pen?!

Don't volunteer to be a victim of the pride bully by not asking someone to help you achieve and do well in your own school of life.

Implementation is the evidence of accountability.

Whose dreams are dying in the waiting room while
you keep dates with procrastination?

If your dream looks like someone else's life, make
sure you are fully aware of all of their challenges,
bad times and nightmares, too.

Breathe. Relax. Enjoy your own lane. Set your own pace. No need to race. The only pace you have to keep up with is the one you set. We'll all get exactly where we're supposed to be. Some sooner, some later, but we'll all get there, if we're not there already.

"For as he thinks in his heart, so is he."
– Solomon, Biblical King of Israel

Giving denies broke.

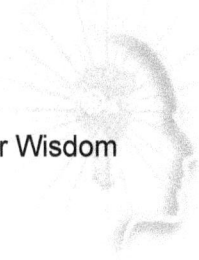

It's okay to be lazy sometimes and it's not lethal to your existence, but it can be genocide to your dreams and goals.

⁂

Be grateful when others are drawn to you and want to do what you do. Because God has given you the grace to make your life look attractive and easy, especially when it isn't.

⁂

It's only drama if you chose to be in the play, and it is obligated to continue and intensify as long as you reward it with the applause of your attention. What drama are you rewarding?

45

Some people will just because it's you. Some people won't just because it's you. All the more reason to keep it easy and just-do-you. There is no other!

⚬⚬⚬

Sometimes "truth juice" can be a little tart. Be sure to make it palatable and serve it with compassion and a genuine smile to sweeten it up a little.

⚬⚬⚬

There is no fear in teaching others what you know. Teaching is how you continue to learn. Just be sure the student is ready.

You won't get all the answers up front. Sometimes,
the additional instructions are wrapped up in
committing to the first yes.

Questions asked reveal your brilliance and answers
become so proud, they let you have them. If you are
afraid or just too cool to ask questions, the answers
feel the same way about you.

The deliberate decision to give removes the
possibility of being "taken."

47

Never underestimate your effectiveness because you
may not hear the immediate applause
from the crowd. There may be silence
because they're actually listening.

Educating the mind without educating the
heart is no education at all.
– Aristotle

Waiting for death to rest in peace would be a grave
mistake, so don't wait to rest in peace, live in it now!

Sometimes the goal isn't achieved by reaching for the next task, but by completing the last one.

Your thoughts; even those that are most divine, are just mental entertainment if they are not lived.

"I absolutely hate when someone listens to me without judgment, because it really bothers me when they think I matter," said no one ever!

If you really want to live life like its golden, be prepared to do the mining and panning.

⸺

You see, while freedom reigns, discipline holds the mirror.

⸺

Courage is the most important of all the virtues, because without courage you can't practice any other virtue consistently. You can practice any virtue erratically, but nothing consistently without courage.
–Maya Angelou

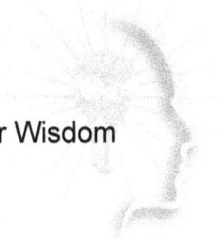

You've heard your problems long enough now it's time those problems listen to you and obey! What do they need to hear from you?

The best proof you have of knowing the answer is living it.

Once you realize (real-eyes) you are enough already, everything else will be too! When enough is enough, it IS!

No moment is ever "off limits" to integrity and excellence, and gratitude for something!

⚜

Peace is not the absence of chaos, it's having the mind-set of not being negatively affected by it.

⚜

You may have to wait for doors to open, so while you're waiting whose door can you be?

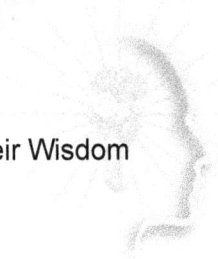

Faith won't come to the job if work doesn't
show up first.

⚜

Don't be limited by being passionate about only
doing one thing. Be passionate about you, and all
you do will include passion.

⚜

You most absolutely do not have to prove what you
are already being!

Laughter is the best medicine. It has the miraculous ability to destroy moments of depression, sadness, anxiety, a bad mood, break the ice and interrupt an argument. You can overdose on it and keep it on a drip if you'd like. Enjoy copious amounts for the euphoric side effects of happiness and instant beautification, and make it contagious.

Laugh often? Laugh often. Laugh often!

All things, yes ALL things considered,
you are still worthy.

Though you may desire support, a witness, or need
encouragement, don't deny your dreams and visions
their right to live by waiting for cosigner.

Only believe what can be, and that's a lot!

⁂

Sometimes the best sense to have is a sense of humor. It is truly medicinal. Hearty laughter can help get you through a painful experience when the situation ain't no joke.

⁂

No, everyone may not like you, but you can deny haters by simply refusing to accept the energy.

Don't worry about being beat by perceived
competition as long as you never lose to YOUrself.
But you may not even have to contend with that
once you decide not to be your own opponent.
You are your greatest, finest and most
qualified cheerleader.

Poor Leaders: Deceptive business practices are the personal lies you dress up to tell. But you will always know you are naked.

Dreams never give up, even if you do, they will find a way to come true.

Life becomes more incredibly amazing when you activate the essence of your spiritual identity.

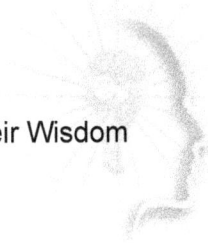

Love waits without weighting.

It may not be a smart idea to speak of how well you know how to get by or struggle, doing so gives those situations reason to stick around to be SURE you get more opportunities, proving your expertise in handling them.

Holding someone accountable for what they never committed to can create emotional debt and bankrupt your relationship.

Time is on your side and procrastination
steals or abuses it.

⚛

"Everybody is a genius. But if you judge a fish by
its ability to climb a tree, it will live its whole life
believing that it is stupid."
– Albert Einstein

⚛

Give an excuse a big relief. Let it go!

When nothing you read seems to work for your situation, it's time to become the living word for what you already know. It's not that the words won't work, they're just depending on you as their example that activates their employment status.

When you create the goal, you can't complain about
the work to be done or choices you have to make
in the process, since your initial decision to
do created them, too.

Yes relationships have architectural definitions,
but not chains.

"Never doubt that a small group of thoughtful and
committed citizens can change the world. It is the
only thing that ever has." – Margaret Mead

Peace isn't just a place of rest it's a place to live in!
Become a permanent resident and a
productive citizen.

Ⓛ

It is enough to think for your own life, don't take
your thoughts to a swap meet that no one else
is showing up for.

Ⓛ

Blaming bears no fruit, not even blaming you!

63

People hearing the best of you is not solely based on what you say or the volume in which you speak, but the sound your life makes as you live it!

❧

You instantly have it all the moment you realize there is nothing missing.

❧

A wedding nor the rings can never determine the value of the relationship, no more than a calendar or a watch gives you time.

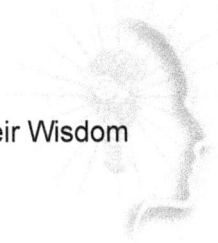

You have to be an enemy to have one.

When it comes to ourselves, some say "Don't judge me" or "Only God can judge me." May we all remember that when we consider the perceived faults of others.

Stop bullying your mind with negative self-talk. Your thoughts are where you create and should never fear being alone with you.

God's most preferred location is everywhere, and no one person, group or belief system has a monopoly on the truth of who God is.

❧

If you can't laugh at yourself, there's someone who is always willing.

❧

"If you want to build a ship, don't drum up the men to gather wood, divide the work and give orders. Instead, teach them to yearn for the vast and endless sea."

– Antoine de St. Exupery

Don't allow your mouth to respond to questions
your life can adequately answer.

Anyone who thinks they have all the answers
hasn't heard all the questions. And, if your life isn't
consistently asking YOU better questions, some
intimidating, you may be living someone else's.

The sooner one discovers and lives their purpose,
the better life becomes for us all!

Humans connect with humans. Hiding
ones humanity and trying to project an
image of perfection makes a person vague,
slippery, lifeless and uninteresting."

– Robert Glover

Yes! God orders your steps, and you get the privilege
and responsibility to plan your ways.

Your life is too big for one person to bear all the
weight. And if you think you can go it alone
and do everything all by yourself, you are
thinking too small.

Love anyway, even if it has to be
different and distant.

No solution will arrive if the problem is never
admitted. Admittance it isn't weakness it's the
beginning of the strength to solve and the
invitation for help to arrive.

Money has every right to be stingy when you are
not generating and earning it doing something
you absolutely love.

Your life exposes the secrets of your
mind's conversations.

You cripple people's return when you don't
make a way for them to invest in themselves.

Worry is like eating bad food and regurgitating it
over and over again. It's gross to the mind! It wastes
so much energy, imagination and time, especially
because the things you worry about usually never
happen. Or you worried about it so much, you
created or attracted it.

Decisions you make, by choice, empower you. But
decisions made by force empower someone else.

71

"Just because a cat has kittens in the oven doesn't
make them biscuits."
– Unknown

No matter how true, wise, profound, or beautiful the
words of others, the words that are most influential
in your life are those you speak to yourself.
What say you?

People can't appreciate you for what they don't
value within themselves.

Relationships only teach wisdom to students who
choose to be wise.

Close the divide between knowing and doing, you're
worthy of the benefits of good work.

How is it possible to live a big life with
little thinking?

Look! If you know you are smart, progressive, and innovative, don't get mad when people can't hang or don't get you right away. Give them time to download your brilliant software. When they look at you strange, or like a mule looking at a new gate, don't take it personal, they're just buffering. There will be times you'll be buffering, too.

Beliefs that are unable to be questioned, are just immature opinions. Beliefs that don't grow into a lifestyle of knowing and foster change, prove they are too weak to live.

All fear is evicted when love owns the house!

Sometimes the face of adversity is only in the thoughts of the face in the mirror.

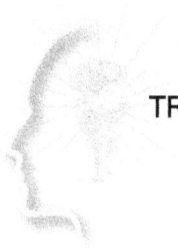

No matter the gender, race, religion, culture or age,
we all want to:

- Be loved

- Belong

- Be heard

- Be valued

- Be appreciated

- Be understood

- Be somebody

"Change will not come if we wait for some other person or some other time. We are the ones we've been waiting for."

–Barack Obama, the 44th President of the United States of America

If you don't like the fish, change the bait!

Everyone is subject to failure, all great people have,
do and will. But their will to succeed overrides
the idea of giving up.

"If you have no confidence in self, you are twice
defeated in the race of life. With confidence, you
have won before you have started."

– Marcus Garvey

Free yourself, it's not so much about what they think anyway; it's about what you believe and live.

Sometimes, you're going to have to pretend to be normal. But, don't be so good at it, and do it as infrequently as possible.

When enough is enough, it is!

"For I know the thoughts that I think toward you, saith the Lord, thoughts of peace, and not of evil, to give you an expected end."
– Jeremiah, The Hebrew Prophet

Wisdom, through purpose, will allow you to know the difference between distractions and opportunities. Behave accordingly.

God wouldn't give you a vision and trick you with lack! God is love and love doesn't work like that!

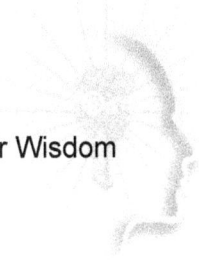

Recognize them, be thankful for them and become
them by sharing them. But if you can ever, literally,
"count" your blessings you are in trouble!

⚬⚭

You can't quit your way to success.

⚬⚭

Thinking does its own work and bears its own fruit.
It is not a substitute for your responsibility to act.

Living your purpose will allow you to know the
difference between people being committed to
YOU versus just being parasitically attached,
or addicted to your benefits.

⌐⟨ℒ⟩⌐

As a leader, sometimes being thought of as crazy is
all the confirmation you need to ensure you
are on YOUR right track.

⌐⟨ℒ⟩⌐

The only difference between being stuck in a rut
and having a successful routine is the
perception of who's in charge.

Greed is an expensive mask paid for by fear.

"Don't set sail using someone else's star."

– African Proverb

"You can't stop a bird from flying over your head,
but you can certainly keep it from building a nest in
your hair. Allow thoughts to come and go, but you
decide which ones take root and grow."

– Walter E. Jones (my dad)

Have a Plan B, but don't make it so attractive that
Plan A is easily aborted.

God only has to "show up" if you think He left.

Leaders, remain teachable. The moment you are
completely comfortable with and have mastered
everything you know, you've stopped learning.

Maybe you've heard it said, "The safest place in the whole wide world is in the Will of God." True! That divine security can only become endangered by you, if "the will" is not executed!

"Before you agree to do anything that might add
even the smallest amount of stress to your life, ask
yourself: What is my truest intention? Give yourself
time to let a yes resound within you. When it's
right, I guarantee that your entire body will feel it."

– Oprah Winfrey

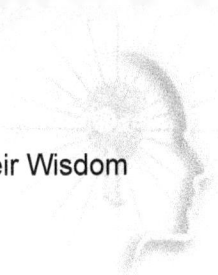

Invest in yourself, you can't afford to
participate in your own depreciation.

Your affirmations that don't bear fruit are
simply rehearsed lies.

Be aware of what seeing you looks like.
You can't control their sight, but you do
determine the view.

Being you is the easiest and most natural job you'll
ever have, so you have no excuse not to show up for
work! Questioning why people want to be with you
or in your presence may prove they know who you
are or have their answer better than you do.

❧

Don't worry about how much you give, your
reSOURCE is infinite, so there is always
more of you where you give from.

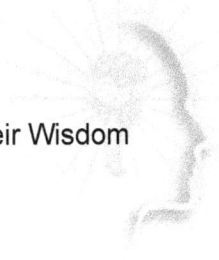

Once you pray and expect an answer, don't despise the how or snub the package the answer comes in.

If you are ashamed to get or ask for help, you'll create the embarrassed solutions, weak results and a dry testimony.

Living on purpose has a way of giving mediocrity, laziness, irrelevance, and stupidity something to complain about amongst themselves.
Keep 'em busy.

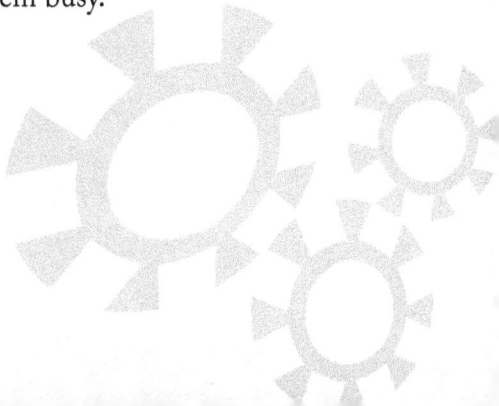

Whenever you're learning, be aware: is it how well they teach or how well they repeat? Are you only accepting of what you already know or have already heard? You can't renew your mind, stuck on the merry-go-round of unfruitful echo chambers.

Any distance between knowing who you are and
being who you are leaves too much
room for insanity!

⚜

True solutions become responsible for themselves.

⚜

The American dream may be a nightmare for you.
You may or may not want the huge house, brand
new car, or 2.5 children. That dream is up for
revision, if you'd like. What's yours?

It's one thing to be forced by change, it's
another thing to cause it.

***

The perception of truth is as unique as the
fingerprint of the person seeing, believing, thinking
or feeling it. How it looks to you may not be
all there is to see.

***

In intimate relationships, no matter how close you
are, oneness doesn't mean you get lost.

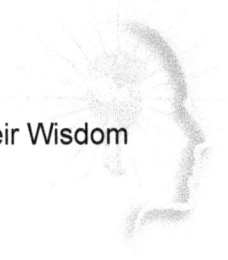

You'll watch your mouth when you realize your
words and thoughts spoken watch you, too.

What is it costing you to stay where you are?

Living on purpose will allow you to become the
answer to someone's prayers, especially
your own. Absolutely!

Having a following doesn't prove you are a leader, that just means you have the ability to attract. One way true leadership can be proven is when those following you have followers, and you genuinely like that. What have your followers created?

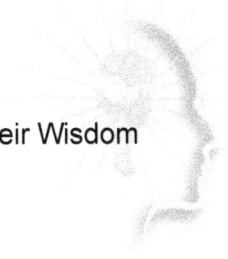

What is the next wonderful thing you'd
like to see happen?

Caress your decisions, with actions, to remind them
that you still love, appreciate and support them.

Don't allow the emotional memory of old offenses
cause you to forget the evidential work of
victory and new triumphs.

Expect to be confronted with problems at the level
of your expertise to solve them.

When you've truly had enough, your realizing
(real-eyes-seeing) YOU ARE ENOUGH will do
something good about it.

Sometimes you wait on a move of God, and
sometimes the move of God is waiting
on you. Move!

It is a self-inflicting wound to expect support for
your purpose from folk who don't know theirs, even
if they are family and friends. Count it as a lesson
learned and surround yourself with purposed-
filled relationships that will.

Our dreams are too valuable for money, alone, to
make their decisions!

Your money needs more than bills to give it
something to do. So, change the responsibility of
your money and give it a do list instead
of a due list, and it will!

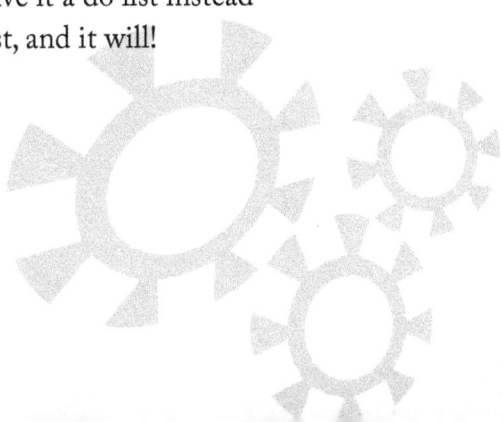

You can't expect "get up" rewards with "sit down"
habits or have "last minute" habits and want
"early bird" results.

It doesn't have to be something loud or big and it
won't require attention or announcement.
But sometimes you can decide and implement
the slightest change that will cause your fears
to be afraid of you.

Don't miss out on your help because you didn't
choose the hand.

Remember, someone is working hard for the things you already have, especially the things money can't buy. Take inventory and be grateful!

─ ✍ ─

Compete with your best moment and WIN!

─ ✍ ─

Celebrate the successes of others as if it were you, because when it comes down to it, it is! It really is! We is me and me is we!

Oh! To be underestimated is a gift!

Relationships operate at the mercy of the speed of trust.

There is absolutely NO honor in being loyal to dysfunction!

Sometimes you can miss your blessing when you argue with or snub the vessel. God's omnipotence isn't limited to your preferences.

Somebody's good news looks just like you.

It doesn't matter who it is, if they won't genuinely help you decorate your life don't let them block your light.

We all say, "God, I thank you for _____!" And
sometimes we have to say, "God, I thank you
for NOT_____!!!

⁂

"You can pray until you faint, but unless you get up
and try to do something, God is not going to
put it in your lap."

– Fannie Lou Hammer

King David, The Psalmist
Psalm 23 The Message (MSG)[1]

23:1-3 God, my shepherd!
I don't need a thing.
You have bedded me down in lush meadows,
you find me quiet pools to drink from.
True to your word,
you let me catch my breath
and send me in the right direction.
4 Even when the way goes through
Death Valley,
I'm not afraid
when you walk at my side.
Your trusty shepherd's crook
makes me feel secure.
5 You serve me a six-course dinner
right in front of my enemies.
You revive my drooping head;
my cup brims with blessing.
6 Your beauty and love chase after me
every day of my life.
I'm back home in the house of God
for the rest of my life.
The Message (MSG) Eugene Peterson

[1]The Message is quoted: "Psalms 23" is taken from The Message. Copyright ©
1993, 1994, 1995, 1996, 2000, 2001, 2002. Used by permission of NavPress
Publishing Group.

Stop! Decide not to give negativity and impossibility
your ideas and imagination.
Make your "what ifs" positive and powerful!

Bold gratitude doesn't give a damn about fear!

Once you know your purpose and begin to
consistently live it you immediately have the privilege
to ask and know the purpose of everyone around you.
Just be ready for the answers or the lack thereof.

Sometimes people will resent you, when because your very presence, alone, reminds them of what they said they wanted to be and do and haven't done. So, even when they choose to be different or distant, love anyway and use wisdom to behave accordingly.

Truth is way too vast and far too brilliant to ever be controlled by one perception.

Just because it's fun, it doesn't mean you're playing.

It's the thought that counts. Yeah, that works for birthdays and Christmas. But when it comes to dreams and visions, the thought that counts is the one that accompanies implementation.

"One of the lessons that I grew up with was to always stay true to yourself and never let what somebody else says distract you from your goals. And so when I hear about negative and false attacks, I really don't invest any energy in them, because I know who I am."
– Michelle Obama

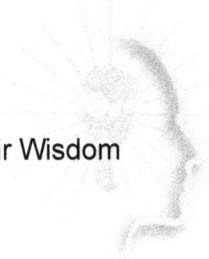

All of your possibilities are waiting on you to decide
their fate. Can they trust you with their lives?

Not only will Truth always prevail, but it's never
offended when tried.

It's okay to be driven as long as it's by you.

The more secretive they stay, the less likely you
are to live them. So holding your life's dreams and
visions hostage in your head will teach them to
reward you the same way.

Knowing that how to listen says it all, and
sometimes that's enough.

Don't put off living or experiencing your greatest
self, right now, waiting to "get to heaven". Because
EVERYwhere God is, IS heavenly...already! And
pure hell is anytime you choose not to believe that.

My brothers and sisters, whatsoever things are
true, whatsoever things are honest, whatsoever
things are just, whatsoever things are pure,
whatsoever things are lovely, whatsoever things
are of good report; if there be any virtue, and if
there be any praise, think on these things.

– St Paul, The Christian Apostle

Don't be fooled, greatness is your birthright and it is
too incredible to wait for fame! Know that you are
great already, no matter who sees it.

The difference between a seed and a tree is growth.
Be willing to start somewhere, on purpose.

IF you want to "take the stage", you must be willing
to climb the stairs.

A "great day" isn't just something you haphazardly
have. It's an opportunity and an agreement with
time that God allows you to create! So having a
great day has a lot to do with your willingness to be
great in it! Be great and enjoy doing great things!

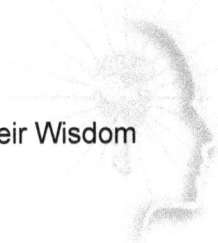

Personal and professional, the value of your relationship is based on the willingness of mutual investment.

Don't offer people your sense, especially when you know they refuse to make change.

Don't have a brilliant mind and mouth with dumb hands. Make your "doing(s)" just as intelligent as your thoughts create and as courageous as your mouth speaks.

You may not know what the day may bring you, but, through purpose, you know what you bring to the day. Rejoice and be glad!

A purposeful relationship is not about "finding" someone to love you. It's about making the inward love for yourself so beautiful, it shows, becomes contagious, and draws out the desire of another to want to join in.

It takes dreams and visions to create goals, but achievement lies in the strategy of the execution.

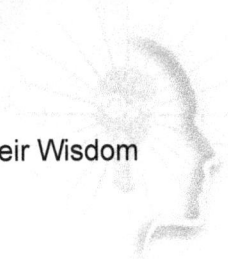

Peace is not a naïve fairy tale. Peace sees chaos and problematic issues and knows they are dead already. THAT Peace, right there, trumps all understanding.

There's no need to identify purpose if you're not going to become what it says. There is no need to seek instructions if you are not going to be obedient to them. What are they saying to you?

Don't be so conditioned to chaos that Peace seems boring.

You are not what happened to you or what you've done—good, bad or indifferent nor are you just the one who lived through it, but you ARE the one who knew you would!

Love makes no credit checks and has no desire for indebtedness.

The outrage of rumors of wars without pales in comparison to any war within. Make Peace with yourself! Doing so automatically authorizes you to have a positive effect on other connected lives and can bring about Universal solutions.

If the problem isn't sugarcoated, don't
sugarcoat the solution.

The attraction, art, sensuality, pleasure, and
satisfaction of sex first happens in mind,
which is your finest.

Knowing who you are comes without explanation or
apology. If you have to explain your position to
get respect, you just lost it.

The best way to know you are necessary is to
appreciate the value in the treasure
of being different.

One of the most radical things you can
do is keep-it-simple.

Don't allow the comforts and luxuries of your
success to become your solitary confinement. Being
imprisoned by things can keep freedom bound, too.

A real entrepreneur is in it because she or he has
no choice. They are dragged by their heart to build
businesses and execute them. They aren't driven by
the money or the current coolness of it... They do it
because they have no choice, not because
it's "hot" right now.

–Gary Vaynerchuk

Resenting having to make decisions may
automatically empower someone else with the
ability to make them for you. Embrace the privilege
to choose and decide; you've been authorized.
What decision do you need to make? What kind of
support to you need to execute?

Your best thoughts and plans are only hindered by
the limitations you give them.

When Peace enters a confused, unfair, a mundane
environment, or a stiff-necked system, initially it
may be perceived as lawlessness and chaos.
Peace isn't still. "Be still" is a command that
chaos obeys in its presence.

Knowing you are enough is incredible. Knowing
what you are enough for...priceless!

119

"No" is impossible when you decide to create or become your own "yes"!

Success is not solely based on how much you can get, but how much you can give without the whispers from the fear of lack.

There is a "ME" in team and there are two "I's" in relationship.

Every great dream begins with a dreamer. Always
remember, you have within you the strength, the
patience, and the passion to reach for the
stars to change the world.

– Harriet Tubman

Love is always in style, purpose is the new
sexy and fun is never overrated!

One of the most beautiful things in the world is to
be firmly embraced and continually secured
by the comfort of a contagious
Self-Acceptance. Accept yourself.

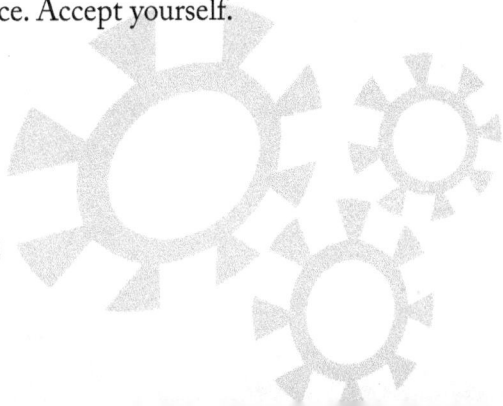

Procrastination allows you to play
stupid with your plan.

Some people are consumed by the same fire you
were purified by and now use to warm your hands.

Change and transition, life is a filled with moments
where something is expiring and another is being
birthed – both unfamiliar, but sure occurrences.

Sometimes doing only will only require you to
listen, be present and be still. Mindfulness.

True gratitude has stamina bolder than the
temporary lifespan of any tangible gift.

Unless you exercise the muscles of
responsibility you will never have the
strength to live in true freedom.

Forget about being taken for granted, facilitate continued peace and promote genuine intimacy in your relationships by not allowing yourself to be privately appreciated and publically ignored.

Teach people how to treat you and use purpose as the lesson plan.

Don't work to get their attention. Enjoy your work, be diligent, and work well and it'll be difficult to ignore you.

Wanna become irrelevant really quick? Keep placating or focusing what you want to say rather than what people need to hear.

⚜

Reading is fundamental, but the application is genius!

⚜

Nobody can sabotage your goals like you can!

Take a good long look in the mirror. Look into your eyes and say, "Thank you for letting me be myself!"

When you genuinely desire something and call out for it with the purest intentions, don't be surprised when it answers more beautifully than you imagined.

If your past comes up to try to bite you, don't be afraid. Live sweetly and make it fall in love with the way you taste now. Let your past know you have no more damns to give!

Answers attract answers, be one!

⚜

True leadership is not measured by quantity, but by
the quality of how those you lead, lead, care for and
instruct their own followers

⚜

Accountability shouldn't be dreaded or feared,
because you're just enlisting volunteers to help
you get the job done and do what you said
you wanted to do. That's empowering!
How much do you want it?

Love does not submit to the dysfunction of pompous entitlements.

Talk about possibilities, decide to create and do new things! Use your happy!

To be touched with the feelings of another's infirmity does not mean you get sick too. It means you live the testimony of how it feels to heal!

Don't quit on you! A goal unattained is an opportunity to discover a new, and improved, way to win.

Relationships you don't have to work at yield no fruit. Remember, the "work" doesn't mean toil, or forced and archaic entitlements, but relationship work means making every conscious effort it takes to lovingly, consistently and willingly show up.

People don't have to use your shoes to prove their mile, nor do you need theirs to prove yours. Enjoy your journey and the privilege of trotting along at your own pace, in your own shoes.

What you can't do is quit on you, and what you can't have is any excuses not to try.

Sometimes the best thing on the other side of a decision is you.

The only thing fear and greatness, inclusion and prejudice, death and life, peace and discontent, love and anger have in common, is they increase at the same momentum, the more you subject yourself to them.

When is the last time you danced or sang out loud?
What's keeping you from doing it?

Once you realize that your spiritual health cannot
be contaminated without your invitation or
consent, you can decide to heal and the do work
of wholeness, and those efforts will fashion your
environment to spread the wealth of health.

Nothing can reveal the quality and the strength of a
relationship, personal or professional, like
great success or serious trouble.

131

Do not take life too seriously. You will
never get out of it alive.

– Elbert Hubbard

Love what you do or ask Wisdom to help you learn
to, or change it if you dare. Because a dreaded hustle
makes miserable money.

Make the decision and make a strategic plan to have
a GREAT day! Repeat.

There is really nothing more to say-except why. But
since why is difficult to handle, one must
take refuge in how.

– Toni Morrison

Your thoughts can't create what you don't believe
and won't violate the willingness of you behavior.

When someone makes love to your body, you may
require exclusivity, and you can have a feel-good
moment. But when someone makes love to your
mind, it's beyond physical. Then, you can make any
moment feel good. Absolutely!

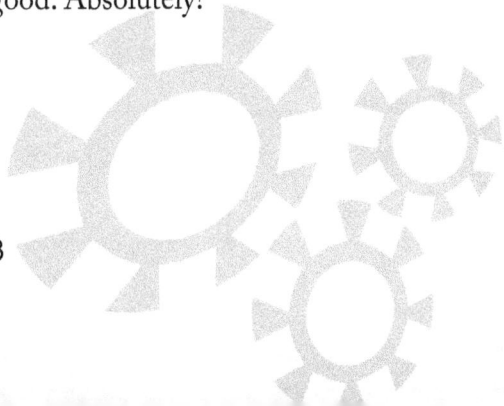

Some of your beliefs have outgrown you because you never believed them 100% anyway.

A perfect God can create no less!

You don't ever have to apologize for loving authentically, your genuine smile, celebrating your hard work, filling the space your gifts made room for, taking time for yourself, guarding your time, enjoying some playtime, letting go of something that hurt, being appreciated and being rewarded or being grateful for healthy the relationships you have. Ain't nothing "sorry" about that, so don't be!

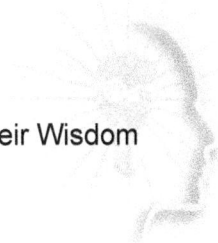

Wisdom teaches you to know the difference when words mean nothing and everything. Say and do what you mean or keep the honor of silence.

⊸❦⊶

Self-discovery isn't selfish. In fact, it's one of the most selfless things you can do, because discovering who you are allows you to love you first that position loves everybody else best. You first, but never you only!

⊸❦⊶

Instead of just asking God to make a way, become the "way" God already made you to be. Show up! You are somebody's provision.

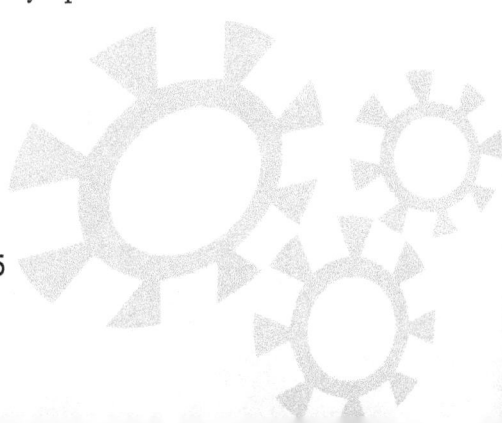

To express generosity without exercising the
wisdom of responsibility is stealing.

Be blessed, friend...God will see you through,
using your eyes to do it.

Your brilliance isn't so much in what you say, but
how consistently you live your own words.

Wrap silence around the words your feet can't walk
out and your heart can't handle receiving
from someone else.

Knowing who you are doesn't mean a thing if you
don't/won't live it! A "knowing" that isn't lived is
ignorance preferred.

The words you speak to your children teach them
what to say to themselves. Your words also teach
them what to think about you.

Trust what you know enough to become it.

***

Peace is not weak! No way! It is a death sentence to chaos and the Grim Reaper to drama and dysfunction! Peace is the order of the day!

***

Sometimes the best way to be heard is to listen.

Heaven is not just a distant "place" where some strive to go after they die. Heaven is also a posture and mind-set of satisfaction and peace that you can operate from. It can be in internal paradise that doesn't accept lack or shortage. It is fulfillment and a genuine satisfaction, an experience with God, in a way that allows gratitude to unselfishly bust at the seams as you light up the world!

Sometimes playing a role behind the scenes is most crucial to the success of the show. But that role is never appropriate when it comes to the production of your own life.

If people continually show you they'd just rather
be without you, allow wisdom to let you know how
quickly your absence can assist them.

Some of your greatest complaints reveal those
things you demand from others and
won't even give yourself.

You already know you don't want to give up on your
dreams, so live life and make decisions in a way that
your dreams won't give up on you!

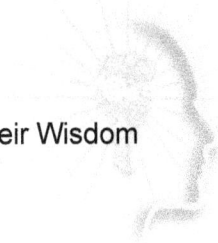

Now you KNOW laziness is intimidated by you
when it breaks character, to work, and seduces you,
to appear attractive.

∝≪ℒ≫⌐

You've heard it said, "What a difference a day
makes." But how about, what a difference you make
to the day! You aren't dependent on a day to be
good to you, the day is depending on you to
be good to it! Act like you're in charge.

You know that "box" you talk about, that you claim you won't let folks put you in? Well, because you authorized the permit to construct, "they" built it using your mind, it's the only place that allows it to exist.

$\approx$

Loving you first loves everyone else best.

$\approx$

By the grace of God, decide to give and receive something great today! Set the intention make sure your gratitude is ready!

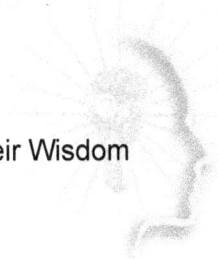

Being like God isn't something you struggle to become, but an identity, responsibility, and way of life you get to accept.

⚶

When your actions put people out of your life, don't act innocent or surprised when they comply and leave.

⚶

People who often say "leave me alone," usually get it.

Pioneers forge ahead and cut down trees so they can walk on through, trailblazers burn 'em down so others can too. Pioneers have the discovery of new territory on their mind, Trailblazers have the progress of nations on theirs. Both are necessary, so just know which one you are, or at least which one you're following.

If you say you love, know that love has no loser behavior. So, if you "do" Love, be about it like a masterful champion.

Allow people to be themselves when they are with
you, whether they like you for it or not.

Its okay to begin again, you now know more than
you did the first time and a fresh start is a win!

Your beliefs, religion, traditions are as
relevant as their ability to evolve.

145

Frequently second guessing yourself brings the
uninvited company of instability and confusion.
When you already know, don't insult your own
intelligence by entertaining the friends
of self-inflicted chaos.

How people treat you is their karma.
How you react is yours.

– Wayne Dyer

If a mistake can kill your mission, that-wasn't-it!

The essence of maturity is allowing yourself to be
held accountable to the privilege of
responsibility you create.

Even in perfect stillness and complete silence,
everything about love is active, alive and well.

If you create incredible value and information for
others that can change their lives—and you
always stay focused on that service—the
financial success will follow.

– Brendon Burchard

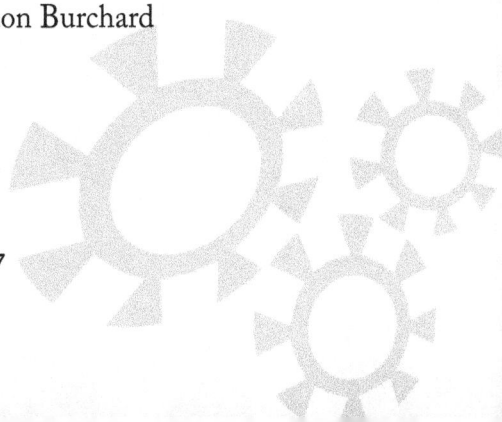

It's something how the same people who
predict it can prevent it.

Success, for you, is whatever you say it is and
what you are willing to do about it, and it's only
limited to the creativity of your defined design and
consistent behavior.

Never allow archaic mind-sets, dogmatic religious
beliefs, and ignorant traditions to rape your mind of
your God-given, spiritual, intelligence.

No one cares if a slave gets rich, as long as the mind
is still enslaved, especially when religion and social
herding are used to provide the shackles.

When you give your dreams a birth date, sometimes
implementing your plans doesn't have a curfew.

Emotions are tools for expression, not masters.

Excuses and achievements come from two, totally different families. Don't adopt excuses when achievements are already in your blood line.

⚓

Don't mistake "fruit" for a big tree with leaves.

⚓

If beauty isn't who you are, what are you looking at?

Societal notoriety is not the qualifier for innate genius and value isn't determined by television cameras, radios and magazines.

Knowing who you are and living your purpose will absolutely ruin your ability to settle for less.

Foolishness is knowledge void of wisdom's application.

Seeds: You do know they become plants, trees, groves and fruit, right? So watch what seeds you put in your mind and mouth. The good ones will grow, especially in the midst of a lot of crap! What type of seeds are you sowing and growing?

Greater is the power of God that lives as you than the humanity people attempt to limit you to.

It is so irresponsible to teach independence without interdependence. Everybody needs somebody, some time, especially because greatness doesn't show up alone and success is much sweeter shared.

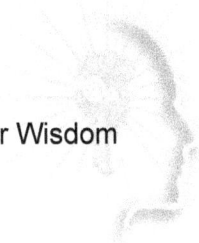

A hushed vision is a dead idea.

❧

The Truth of God is far too omniscient for you and
yours to be the only ones to know it and
express it the "right" way.

❧

If you put God first, you've reduced your perception
of God to the level of being prioritized along with
the rest of your stuff. God first? No, baby,
God only. Always. Everything.

If you keep feeling like you owe it, you do.
Don't tarry!

Most of your battles lost never left your mind, so no
one else had a chance to say a thing before you have
already thought your way out of a win. You may
already have to contend with doubt and argument
from the outside, so by all means at least
agree with yourself!

"In the twenty-first century, the best anti-poverty
program around is a world class education."

–Barack Obama, the 44th President of the
United States of America

The difference between a trick and a
surprise is motive.

Don't ever allow anyone to possess or determine
what makes you beautiful. The essence of what
makes you beautiful is the freedom to be so.

Excellence you expect or demand from others is the same excellence required of you!

Your "yes" or "no" is enough. No need to make up reasons, waste your imagination to create excuses or employ fear to help you create lies. Yes. No. Enough.

In truth, there is a huge difference between one
thought, one mind, and one idea vs. one brain.
Learn from your teachers, but by all means, you are
ultimately responsible to think for yourself! The
spirit of oneness and the idea of being unified
is not at all related to mind control,
groupthink and being brainwashed.

Goodness and mercy are easy to give once you
realize how much they've had your back.

You can delegate your words to serve others but
you cannot make them taste and eat. Just be sure to
consume and digest your own statements of service.
It's the evidence that your own nutritional
value supports your livelihood. Your
quality of life depends on it.

Know the difference between getting
used and being used.

Can love trust you to be it? Can life trust you to live it? Can your gift trust you to give it? Can prosperity trust you to grow it and success trust you to show it? Can who you are trust you to know it? And can all of that trust you to do it? How?

Don't be flattered by people who continue to be satisfied with crumbs when you've offered to help them make their own bread. They'll eventually begin to want your loaves, without the effort of at least being in the kitchen. Don't enable malnourishment as a lifestyle or default. It's time to be better and do greater.

"When your clarity meets your conviction and you apply action to the equation, your world will begin to transform before your eyes."

– Lisa Nichols

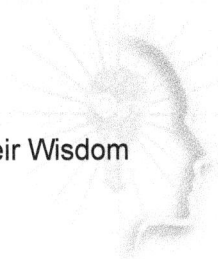

Don't try so hard to get into a relationship, work on being relatable and enjoy people for who they are, and relationships show up effortlessly!

∞

"Your power is in your thoughts, so stay awake. In other words, remember to remember."

– Rhonda Byrne, *The Secret*

∞

Do you realize your repeated thoughts and words are so powerful they MUST manifest? What's is happening with you is the fruit of your own thinking, speaking, and behaving, and if you are experiencing challenges, your creative mind can design a way to overcome.

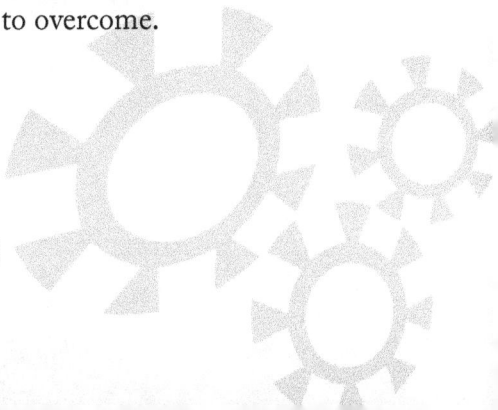

Remember when you are observing the edited
lives of others, just because they're talking about it,
doesn't mean its happening.

Speak when you are angry, and you will make the
best speech you'll ever regret.

– Laurence J. Peter

Let's keep it real, businesses that don't invest in
their people suck! People don't leave companies
they flee bad management.

What would it mean or how would you feel if you were able to change the thing(s) about you that have been the most challenging?

⸎

"What we need now, more than anything else, are people who are willing to do the difficult work of bridging gaps and healing wounds, people in our communities who can rally others together, across lines of division, for the greater good..."[1]

– Cory Booker, United States Senator

[1]*United: Thoughts on Finding the Common Ground and Advancing the Common Good* by Cory Booker, Copyright 2016, Publisher: Random House Books, New York, Ballentine Books

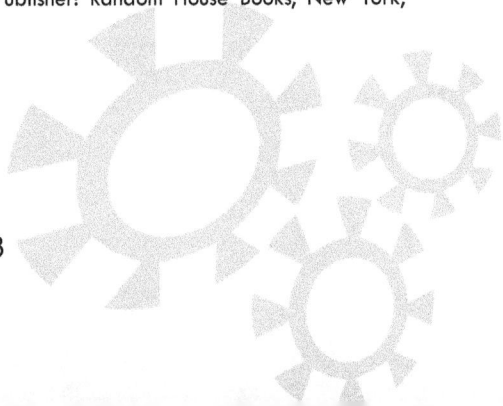

Solomon, The Wise King
Proverbs 3:13-18 Message (MSG)[2]

You're blessed when you meet Lady Wisdom,
when you make friends with Madame Insight.
She's worth far more than money in the bank;
her friendship is better than a big salary.
Her value exceeds all the trappings of wealth;
nothing you could wish for holds a candle to her.
With one hand she gives long life,
with the other she confers recognition.
Her manner is beautiful,
her life wonderfully complete.
She's the very Tree of Life to those who embrace
her. Hold her tight—and be blessed!

The Message (MSG) Eugene Peterson
[2]The Message is quoted: "Proverbs 3: 13-18" is taken from The
Message. Copyright © 1993, 1994, 1995, 1996, 2000, 2001,
2002. Used by permission of NavPress Publishing Group.

Tracy "TracyMac" McNeil

As result of working with 12-Year Relationship Management Expert, Tracy "TracyMac" McNeil, Fortune 500 companies, executive suite professionals, coaches, institutes of higher learning and government agencies, experience the exceptional value of having an expert relationship strategist and a confidant to help mastermind solutions. She collaborates with her clients as they consistently experience accelerated wins in every area.

Through self-discovery, personal & professional development, leadership effectiveness training and seminars, they up-level and add momentum to their purpose, mission and passion, saving them time to consistently enjoy healthy relationships, increase influence and boost revenue! As a certified mediator of MTI Eckerd College, she blends her twenty-eight years of experience with federal, state and local governments, non-profit organizations and being an ordained teacher into her expertise as a certified, professional, she became a life coach in 2004 while living in Okinawa Japan.

The founder of Peace Place LLC, TRACYMAC Coaching Services and TRACYMAC Publishing, she also attended Winston Salem State University and later earned her degree in Behavioral Science from Western International University, graduating Magna Cum Laude. She is a graduate and certified coach of Coach Training Alliance and received a certification, as a Master Life Strategist with the KAIROS Institute of Personal Discovery.

TracyMac's philanthropic efforts support numerous nonprofit organizations, veterans and mental health organizations and as an active board member "Families Together," she rigorously supports, gives to and spearheads fund raisers for homeless children and families. As an Amazon Bestselling author, her books are setting positive change ablaze within personal and professional relationships. TracyMac lives in Raleigh, North Carolina with her husband of 23 years, Owen and their daughter Jayda.